Magma

the lightning flash ⚜ the electric spark in the dark ⚜ the shooting star burst of brilliance ⚜ the impulse ⚜ rising from the deep ⚜ formless thought ⚜ echoing from a hollow place ⚜ temptation ⚜ compelling curiosity ⚜ a vital longing ⚜ fuel for the trajectory ⚜ into flights of imagination ⚜

Figment **Books**

Other titles in this series:

Wellspring

In a Grain of Sand

Available through www.figmentcreativity.com

Figment Books

An Imprint of Figment Creative Expression Ltd.

Copyright © 2019 by Laura Turnbull Fyfe

www.figmentcreativity.com

Printed in the UK.

ISBN 978-1-912099-72-6

A CIP record for this book is available from the British Library.

Contents

Magpie Mind 1
with a contribution from Charlie Gracie

Golden Key 11
with a contribution from Janice Galloway

Panning for Gold.. 19
with a contribution from Liam Murray Bell

Filling Your Nest 35
with a contribution from Lesley Traynor

Smooth Your Feathers 61
with a contribution from Tom Leonard

Magpie in the Mirror 73
with a contribution from Alan Bissett

Of Magpies and Monkeys 85
with a contribution from Emma Mooney

A Warning: The Gilded Cage 93
with a contribution from Chris Powici

Resistance 103
with a contribution from Leonie Charlton

Final Call 117
with a contribution from Stuart Paterson

Prompts 121

Note of Thanks 132

Recommended Reading 134

Magpie Mind

What is it about mountains that compels us to climb them? Why do we pull on our walking boots and push through the cold and the pain of straining thighs and burning lungs? Perhaps it's the challenge they pose. We want to know we can do it. That we can conquer them, stand on their summits and know we've achieved something great.

It's that, but it's also more than that. It's the pull of the unknown, the unexplored, the drive to experience something new. It's adventure.

Though… we don't just climb mountains to see what it's like up there. We also climb to look at where we've been. We wonder how the landscape of our life will look from that heady fresh-air perspective, and how we will feel once we're up there.

Curiosity. That's our inner Magpie.

Magpies have been the scapegoats of the bird kingdom for centuries. They're often accused of swooping down and flying off with anything shiny they can get their talons on. This, sadly, is a myth, but it's no less bewitching for its fiction. I use this idea in workshops and now here, to describe spontaneous creativity and emphasise the importance of having a 'magpie mind'.

In other words, like magpies, let's be open to opportunity. Let's seize on those little moments of creative sparkle that occur in our lives. I don't mean the overt kind of bling that stops you in your tracks as you pass a jewellery store window. Consider, rather, the subtle glint of something shiny in the undergrowth. A formless thought, a possibility that tantalises the edge of your consciousness and says: *there's* something interesting.

> **Poems are responses to needs, urges, hungers, thirsts, they have sprouted forth.**
> **– Glyn Maxwell**

It's the light bulb, the lightening flash, the electric spark in the dark that ignites the imagination.

> **A star falls from the sky and into your hands. Then it seeps through your veins and swims inside your blood and becomes every part of you.**
> **– C. Joy Bell**

These experiences are catnip to writers and artists, scientists too – bursts of brilliance that shouldn't be ignored. Daydreams and crazy schemes that, when we wear our grown-up hats, we ignore. As adults, we often have far more important things to think about – like bills and mortgages. How dull.

> We are traditionally rather proud of ourselves for having slipped creative work in there between the domestic chores and obligations. I'm not sure we deserve such big A-pluses for that.
> – Toni Morrison

For those who want to create, stamping out these urges is soul-destroying. Some even believe that such stifling of creativity can cause depression. I'm not sure if it goes so far as to set off this life-crippling illness, but I know my life is certainly more fulfilling when I'm writing. I walk lighter, breathe more easily. Repressing the very human yearning to create can cause great unhappiness.

> Writing is survival... you must stay drunk on writing so reality cannot destroy you. – Ray Bradbury

Many artists, regardless of their medium, find that if they do not engage with and act upon their creative drive on a regular basis, they feel deeply, spiritually unfulfilled.

> We do not write because we want to; we write because we have to.
> – Somerset Maugham

For some, life will never be enough unless they are able, at least sometimes, to act on their creative compulsions. And one project is rarely enough, because the desire to craft something new can only be temporarily, if ever, satisfied.

> **As artists, we are spiritual sharks. The ruthless truth is that if we don't keep moving, we sink to the bottom and die.**
> – Julia Cameron

It's in the process of creation that we find fulfilment, not in the completion. We enjoy learning, and while we might initially feel intimidated by the time and effort involved, or worry that we might not be capable, we realise at some point that this challenge is where the fun lies. Once it's done, it's dull. And so on to the next artistic fix.

> **When we get there, there disappears... we are once again confronted with our creative self and its hungers.**
> – Julia Cameron

If I go too long without writing, I become very grumpy. Homicidally grumpy. My chiropractor can always tell if I've been writing or not. If I *have* been writing, there tends to be very little correction needed for my spine. I stand taller, happier, as if the energy of creation has shored me up. You might find you feel the same way.

These spontaneous moments of inspiration beguile and bewitch all who love the thrill of a new idea, and even tempt those who normally consider themselves too sensible for such frivolity. The potential for revelation is there in all of us. Any absence of these phenomena is death to writers, artists and innovators.

> **It is this experience of tapping some magic source that makes the writer an addict, willing to give up almost anything for his art, and makes him, if he fails, such a miserable human being.**
> **– John Gardner**

Opening your imagination to the ideas and insights that your subconscious (or Muse) presents to you can be life-changing. Even world-changing. It's these flashes of illumination that enrich our very existence – why would we let them go to waste?! It's these vivid messages from we-know-not-where that provide solutions for the puzzles and diversion from the problems in our lives. These instinctive fascinations make life interesting. They compel us to take our imaginations on unprecedented adventures. If we're courageous enough to follow them. Geniuses around the world, throughout time, have relied on these moments of revelation for their discoveries. Why not you?

> These bizarre moments, sometimes thrilling, sometimes just strange, moments setting off an altered state, a brief sense of escape from ordinary time and space – moments no doubt similar to those sought by religious mystics, or those experienced by people near death – are the soul of art, the reason people pursue it.
> – John Gardner

So I say: play.

If want the creative side of yourself to come to greater prominence, then you're going to want these moments of insight to happen more often. This book is designed to help you find them.

If my advice works for you, you won't be able to stop yourself. Who knows how high your *Magpie Mind* might soar? *Bon voyage*, and *bon chance!*

Charlie Gracie

It's nearly always the mountains. Being up there, of course, but among them, seeing them at a distance, everything they are.

On top of a mountain, alone, you feel completely part of the enormous world.

A path, shuffled along and trodden, is the earliest sign of human interaction with the earth. Like all our engagement with it and each other, following the path is a guide, but something we add to as well, our steps confirming the way for everyone else who comes after. For the best of the mountains but, I like to get off the path, slog through heather, slide down snow, wade over burns: this is where poems and stories be.

In the mountain, everything is monumental, even a tiny pearlwort flower, the tst tst of a pipit; in the mountain, every-thing is almost nothing, even the highest crag, the deepest corrie.

The mountains hold all their elemental, creative energy in them, and in quiet moments on the windswept sides of any hill you can close your eyes and breathe that energy in.

I don't ever write when I'm on a mountain. I just let it all seep into me and work away until it is ready to come out.

Golden Key

A golden key can open any door. Once you've opened yourself to the world around you, the possibilities you will find there are infinite.

As children, in school, we're discouraged from daydreaming, from scribbling, from doodling. Our thoughts are forced between lines and inside boxes. As we grow up, all too often the critical, logical sides of our minds are valued over the creative, simply because the objective retention and recall of facts can be more easily measured in exams and entered on CVs as evidence for our employability. Is it any wonder, then, that the creative sides of our minds become suppressed.

At least now, in education, our abilities to analyse and interpret are developed. But the highest order, the most advanced and elusive brain function – creativity – is so difficult, so subjective to judge that it cannot be easily assessed, and is thus rarely considered in our results-driven society. And so the encouragement of creativity, a skill increasingly vital to our society, continues to be sidelined. Is it any surprise, then, that when our Muses tentatively tap at our doors, they are often ignored?

> By the time many people are fourteen
> or fifteen, they have been divested of
> their loves, their ancient and intuitive
> tastes, one by one, until when they reach
> maturity there is no fun left, no zest, no
> gusto, no flavour. Others have criticised,
> and they have criticised themselves, into
> embarrassment.
> – Ray Bradbury

Instead of shutting out your insights and ideas, I ask you to write them down. Immediately. Even if you are struggling for time or in the middle of some task that requires your undivided attention, note the idea down very briefly on whatever you have to hand: a phone, a post-it note, a napkin, or on the back of your hand. If you happen to be driving, pull over and jot it down before continuing on your journey. Put that idea into words as soon as you can.

> It is necessary to write, if the days are
> not to slip emptily by. How else, indeed,
> to clap the net over the butterfly of the
> moment? For the moment passes, it is
> forgotten; the mood is gone; life itself is
> gone. That is where the writer scores over
> his fellows: he catches the changes of his
> mind on the hop.
> – Vita Sackville-West

You have to be ready. Hang a sail out in your mind to harness every gust of inspiration. Open a net to catch those thoughts that might otherwise flutter by. Turn your surfboard in the right direction so you're ready to ride the next swelling wave.

Often, the truly great ideas and descriptions are the ones you observe in the present, not the ones you write about from your past. Of course, it is still possible to write well from memory, but why struggle with recall when you can use a description that you've taken down in a perfect moment? Much easier!

Give yourself permission now for your imagination to become a priority. Are you courageous enough to set everything else aside for a few minutes? That's all it takes to jot down the sketch of an idea. Once you decide to note down your insights, observations and reflections in this way, you're committing yourself to a new, more creative way of living. Once you've written something down it becomes real, no longer just some lofty idea that you might one day write about. Accept that you might not ever be able to turn it into a fully-fledged masterpiece. The real victory lies in facing yourself, your skills and limitations as a writer – and about actually *writing!*

Dedicating a few minutes of your time to this whenever it happens will mark a crucial shift in your creative process. You're no longer a dentist or teacher or nurse who also writes. You're a writer (or artist) who does those other things in between their writing.

> **Because there is a natural storytelling urge and ability in all human beings, even just a little nurturing of this impulse can bring about astonishing and delightful results.**
> **– Nancy Mellon**

The most thrilling thing about making the decision to note down every creative urge you receive is that the more open you are, the more you act on your impulse to create, the more often this impulse will occur. Get into the habit of welcoming your Muse when she knocks on your door and you'll find she comes to visit much more frequently.

The golden key is the permission you give yourself – and it's the only tool you need to open your mind to infinite inspiration.

Janice Galloway

Inspiration...some rely on it absolutely and others deny it ever touches their 'imagination'.

(though where that imagination comes from is not adequately addressed if it's not memory...)

...The idea to garner ideas on ideas - inspiration to some, random thought process to others - is of course a great idea. If only we had more words for ideas we might talk about it more.

Panning for Gold

Magpies are not only intelligent, they're opportunists. It's one of the reasons they thrive, particularly in urban areas where many other species struggle. They have a broad diet and adapt very well – habits that we can borrow to help our creative instincts flourish.

The wider your interests, the broader your torch-beam of curiosity, the more chance you have of finding that glint of treasure in the darkness.

> One of the arts of the poet is to make comprehensible and articulate what might emerge from subconscious sources; one of the great main uses of the intellect is to select, from the amorphous mass of subconscious images, those that will best further his imaginative purpose.
> – Dylan Thomas

Think of it as panning for gold. Not all the ideas you gather will turn out to be gold – and you might have to sort through quite a few pebbles and shards to find them. All the more reason to keep looking. The more ideas you can produce, the better the chances are that you'll be successful with at least one of them. As Nobel Prize winner Linus Pauling said, 'The best way to have a good idea is to have lots of them'. Reframe your thinking: measure your imagination's success by the number of unique ideas you've had that day, not by the 'quality' of them.

> **Ideas are like rabbits. You get a couple
> and learn how to handle them, and pretty
> soon you have a dozen.**
> – John Steinbeck

To stack the odds in your favour, it's vitally important to take your critical voice out of the equation. Don't dismiss anything – there'll be plenty of time to sift through it all later so you can pick out what glitters and work with it.

If an idea doesn't immediately strike you as wonderful, keep it anyway and put it off to one side. It may be a partial solution to a future creative conundrum. The process of alchemy takes time. Be patient and let this happen.

Above all, the very best way to encourage creativity is to create. The more you do so, the more ideas will come to you.

Stay open. Try new things. Below, I'm going to offer a few suggestions to help you fill your metaphorical sieve from that fast-moving stream of creativity.

Some of these will be familiar. Others you'll not have tried before. If you feel resistance to any of them, acknowledge that and consider why you feel that way. Might it actually be a resistance to change in your life? Change can be scary, after all. But what would you really stand to lose in giving each of them a try? Adapt them to your schedule and writing practice in different ways to suit yourself. Experiment to see what might work best. Every single one of them is included here because of the overwhelming evidence that they boost creativity.

You may strain against the confines of a daily practice. Establishing a routine may risk turning something you enjoy into a chore. Persevere.

But if, after sustaining a regular practice for a few weeks, it's still not working for you, then stop. Don't risk stifling your creativity. Do whatever works for you to ensure inspiration ignites as often as possible. Nothing will fire you up if you remove your flame from the oxygen that feeds it.

Diary

As with your *Wellspring* writing, in your diary you can be completely honest. A diary is a trusted friend with whom you can pour out all your heartbreak and heart's desires without fear of judgement or the need to self-censor. Not only is diary writing cathartic, it can provide material for a potential autobiography.

Diary-writing also provides a character that you can adapt for future novels. I wonder to what degree each character in a novel is really just a facet of the writer's own personality anyway. Most writers do, consciously or unconsciously, base their main characters to some extent on people they know – after all, to make them real to the reader they must be able to identify with them.

And then, of course, writing a diary is a perfect way of collecting those special moments in your life that might otherwise drift away on the sands of time. In writing a diary, you compile a treasure chest of glinting gold coins, each stamped with your own face. And you provide a means to reflect on how you've changed and developed and grown as you've aged.

You might worry that that there's no value in your writing. Stop worrying. Start valuing yourself. The experiences you write about will be completely unique because no one else has lived your life.

That's what makes them valuable. But they will also be completely sympathetic, because they'll be honest and human – and so every human reading will be able to empathise to some extent. That's what makes them relevant.

Wellspring writing is all about quick-fire inspiration and breaking down your blocks, but writing a diary provides the opportunity for slow, soul-deep reflection. In a diary you can explore yourself and your experiences in a completely different way. If you take your time and write more slowly, you may achieve a flow and depth that you do not achieve at any other time. It's worth experimenting with different paces, styles and focuses. When writing in your diary, perhaps reflect on something you've experienced that day:

> a friend, an enemy or stranger
> an old routine or habit
> a particular moment
> a new experience
> a new passion
> an old fear
> a lesson

The Process Log

Henriette Anne Klauser, in her excellent book *Writing on Both Sides of the Brain*, recommends that every day, you chart your course and your progress "as a writer". Make note of the date and time of your entry and then free-write in order to record information about what happens as you write, your aspirations and your progress towards those aspirations – perhaps stories about how you learned to write, as well as successes, challenges and 'failures'.

Klauser recommends this process because it helps a writer notice patterns about what impedes and supports them in their processes, helping them identify strengths and weaknesses, and sort through ideas. It also encourages moments of spontaneous flow.

Be open-minded about what might happen in your process log and where it might lead you.

A Daily *Wellspring* Practice

Experiment with your *Wellspring* practice:

- use random prompts such as those at the bottom
  of the pages in *Wellspring*
- use random ideas related to a project you're
  working on to help you explore that project from
  different perspectives
- use your *Magpie Mind* findings as prompts
- freewrite using prompts to scavenge your
  memories and reflections on life, the universe
  and everything.

Using prompts to help you explore your life and your
ideas might feel too easy. When you read back over what
you've written, you might feel it's too simplistic. But of
course it will seem easy – it's come straight from your
head. I guarantee someone else reading it will feel quite
differently. This comes up time and again at writing
workshops. We all see the value in each others' writing
so much more than in our own. Try not to be too harsh
on yourself.

> One must be capable of allowing the
> darkest, most ancient and shrewd parts
> of one's being to take over the work from
> time to time. Or be capable of cracking the
> door now and then to the deep craziness of
> life itself.
> – John Gardner

At some point in your *Wellspring* writing there'll come a moment when, while digging around for something to write about, you hit a vein of gold. You suddenly realise that this, here, is something you can really dig down into, something you can't help but write.

Gabriele Lusser Rico, in *Writing the Natural Way*, calls this the trial-web-shift, when you move beyond stitching your web of ideas together and shift spontaneously into creating a pattern of your own. At first, you'll be brainstorming a random list of associations, and then you suddenly find a sense of direction, you may feel tentative at first, and then you get into your groove like a needle finding the tune on an LP. Then, with that new sense of purpose, you'll release any tensions and doubts and feel yourself opening up to your burst of insight – an irresistible impulse to write, an exhilaration that settles into a contented satisfaction that you won't want to end.

Don't stop until your pen stops. Let the figment of your imagination become reality.

Early Birds

Of all the suggestions I give to writers, this one encounters the most resistance. Nothing rivals the gaping looks of horror I receive from self-professed night-owls when I suggest that getting up even ten minutes earlier to write might be a great way to begin each day.

If you're so sleepy that you keep hitting your snooze button, one might perhaps suggest that you need to go to bed a little earlier. Honestly, what's the big deal when the benefits you could reap far outweigh a few more minutes of alarm-clock-disturbed tossing-and-turning?

Why not just start the way you mean to go on? I tend to do my morning writing over a cup of tea. I set up my notebook and pen while the kettle's boiling. Dorothea Brande goes one further and suggests you write without having done anything else at all first, before your mind becomes diluted by the day's preoccupations. Get up earlier than you're used to: a half hour, even an hour, and write straightaway!

Writing first thing in the morning is a formula recommended in many writing guides, including Julia Cameron's *The Artist's Way*. Many writers prefer to do most of their writing in the early hours (Haruki Murakami at 4am, for example) so that they're closer in mindset to their dreaming mind, to their subconscious. Writing early, even before dawn, before the world wakes up, takes on a magical, womb-like quality, private and undisturbed by sensible, logical thoughts of the impending day.

If you begin your day by writing, you also increase your chances of that story or poem staying with you, percolating away in the background of your consciousness until you get the chance to return to it.

Klauser found that the more she and her work-shoppers did this, the more it increased their output: 'you have at your fingertips more than double, even triple the amount of output of the day before. Your writing will have an energy and flow that incorporates all the mental, possibly unconscious musing of the twenty-four hours in between.'

Just try it! *

* of course, for the sake of argument, also experiment with writing last thing at night.

An idea is a bit of grit under the skin. You're not sure how it got there, but you scratch at it and it either goes away or it imbeds itself further. You need to itch it some more. The skin around it gets irritated, but you break through and draw some clean, red blood. The itch is worse than ever, so you keep scratching and you pick and pull and prod at it.

At that stage, you take it to someone else to show them, to ask their advice. They tell you how to squeeze out the white and yellow pus. They press at the scab, to see if it will ooze. Perhaps, even, they offer you stitches to tie it together, to keep it contained.

After a few weeks, the itch has lessened. It just needs a light scratch every day and some ointment in the evenings. You know, if it came to it, you could open the wound right up again. You don't need to, though, because you've got this beautiful shiny scar, perfectly formed, over that piece of grit.

And that's when you're ready to sit down and write.

Filling Your Nest

Beginnings

Take a line from a movie, a novel, a song, a poem, a proverb or cliché – any phrase or sentence that catches your interest. Adapt it a little to make it your own and use that to begin your writing.

In a similar vein, I love the programme Blankety Blank. There are so many ways a phrase or sentence can be turned into something funny and imaginative if you just take out a key verb or noun and replace it with something else. Try this when you're stuck for inspiration and use it to get you started (check the prompts section at the back of this book for suggestions).

Connections

Free association is a great way of brainstorming ideas and is one that psychologists since Freud have used to recover memories and explore the ways their patients think.

Ray Bradbury used single nouns as titles with which to explore his imagination. Tony Buzan, on the other hand (an expert in the organisation and exploration of ideas, who coined the phrase 'mind-map') suggests that it is easier to get your brain sparking by creating connections between things rather than trying to start your engine up cold with just one idea.

> **Everything in some way connects to everything else.**
> **– Leonardo Da Vinci**

For example, give yourself a minute to try to think up ten uses of a brick (do this first before reading on)…

…

Now try to think up ten uses of a brick in the following situations or with these objects: a locked room, a bookcase, a lightbulb, a clock, a pile of papers, a set of scales, a fire, a nut, a swimming pool, a garden, a mobile phone, a door and a pen.

I bet that was much easier!

Ted Hughes did the same with his students. He would give them pairs of opposites, or pairs of apparently unrelated words, then ask them to brainstorm (or mind-map or free-associate) five to ten words around each. He would then ask them to find connections between the words produced on each opposite side. According to Buzan, 'Many of the associations were extremely unusual, highly imaginative, very provocative, and often quite moving.'

So when you're struggling for ideas, have a look around and instead of getting ideas from one object, link two different things and see where that takes you. And when you're making those connections, don't try to force it, don't concentrate. Relax. Unfocus your eyes, unfocus your mind, and use your soft gaze. See the prompt section at the end of this book for suggestions to get you started.

Deadlines

Having a sense of purpose greatly increases the odds of coming up with something that isn't only original but is also worthwhile. Sign up to email newsletters, look at the Facebook pages and Twitter feeds of writing magazines, journals, zines, and blogs for their competitions and submission deadlines.

Put these dates on a calendar or on your phone (with reminders and alerts so you have some lead time) to ensure you don't miss out on opportunities.

Join writing groups, workshops or courses, online or in person, so you can be given a little direction and motivation in the form of writing exercises.

Dream Diary

As with the *Wellspring* and *Magpie Mind* processes, the more you write in your dream diary, the more it'll work for you. Write in your dream diary as soon as you wake up to help you remember your dreams more often and more vividly. They're right there – you might as well use them!

Keep a notebook by the side of your bed to write in. Note down the ideas that pop up just as you're dropping off. You know, the ones: those you tell yourself you'll remember when you wake up – and never do. Then write your unconscious dreams down the next morning.

Dreams and nightmares have offered artists and thinkers a font of inspiration for millennia. Paul McCartney (who I'm listening to right now as I write – how's that for synchronicity?) said he wrote *Hey Jude* immediately upon waking up. Margaret Atwood's *Alias Grace* came from a dream about having written an opera about a nineteenth-century emigrant called Suzanna Moodie. So she researched it, wrote a poem, a television play, then the novel. Stephen King was inspired by a childhood nightmare to write *Salem's Lot*.

If it's good enough for them, it might be worth a shot.

Follow your Fears

One of the best pieces of writing advice that I've ever received was to face my fears. Immediately my stories became much more visceral – and more human. It upped the stakes for my characters and made them instantly more identifiable and sympathetic.

Conflict gives your writing energy, so use your own fears and worries to provide your characters with internal conflict.

> **Writing is turning one's worst moments into money.**
> – J. P. Donleavy

Remember it's suffering that makes us human (according to Buddhist doctrine), and we suffer as a result of our fears, so use your own fears to imbue your plots with scary situations and difficult decisions for your character.

Listen

Pay attention to things around you – in a relaxed and passive way. Be present, be open to whatever happens, without judging or thinking one way or another.

> **Listening is receptivity. The deeper you**
> **can listen, the better you can write.**
> **– Natalie Goldberg**

In his famous list of prose essentials, Jack Kerouac advises writers to be submissive to everything. Trust in the process, in your *Magpie Mind,* or Muse or subconscious, whatever you prefer to call it. Ideas will flare without you having to do very much to kindle them. It's usually very peaceful, and always interesting.

> **It is like fishing. But I do not wait very**
> **long, for there is always a nibble – and this**
> **is where receptivity come in... Something**
> **always occurs, of course, to any of us. We**
> **can't keep from thinking.**
> **– William Stafford**

Look

Look again. Look differently. Through one eye, then the other. Blink.

Look where you've not looked before, up to roof-tops, up to the dome of the sky. Cloud-gaze, enjoy the play of light on rain-showers, look at the ground, look around. Look at people you don't know and wonder about the life that lives beyond their surface. Look at those you know – people you like. What might be their flaws? Look at people you don't like and try to understand where they're coming from. Look at people you love and wonder at their quirks and their qualities. Consider their motivations, strengths, weaknesses, challenges.

In a conflict, play devil's advocate and look at all sides of the encounter.

Look at a picture or object and imagine what it could be as opposed to what it actually is. This can release a fresh train of thought (*Mind Gym*, Time Warner Books).

When you see a set of handlebars and a bicycle seat, you might fill in the blanks (a frame, wheels, chain and so on) and think of a bicycle – but Picasso created his *Bull's Head*. Upcyclers do this very thing to great effect – who would think of making a chair out of an old tin bath? But they can look great. Though I'm not sure how comfortable one would be...

Looking, for some reason, is a more active verb than listening. Flit between the two, looking and listening, thinking and observing.

Memories

We write memoir to relive and relieve. We write so we don't forget, so we're not forgotten. We write to free ourselves. We write to hold on. We write to release.

If a memory pops up, explore it. It's probably come back to you for a reason. Trust your instincts, your subconscious and follow where the memory leads you.

Writing memoir is another way to examine how our mind works. To observe how we think, how we once thought, and how we've changed.

Use *Wellspring* writing and free-association to help with this. These are great tools for trawling through your past. Create connections between your experiences to generate new ideas.

Metaphor and Symbol

The way that metaphor works reveals a wonderful aspect of the human mind. It's not always linear or logical. When we think of a candle, we might think of what a candle is: wax and a wick. We also think of what it does: when lit it provides light. But, more interestingly, along with that idea of what a candle is and does are ideas about what the candle represents. We use them when praying in church, when sitting at a table in a nice restaurant, when relaxing. So a candle can also represent hope, religion, love, romance, indulgence or relaxation.

Each symbol or metaphor holds different significance for each person. A cat for some people represents comfort, home, affection and softness. Others associate cats with threat, claws and teeth, glowing eyes and malignancy.

Use your imagination: what could you compare each inanimate object to? Its shapes, textures, and so on. Go further by describing a certain process or object, then compare it to another, for example:

- Describe a train journey – now compare it to childbirth.
- Describe playing a set of drums – now compare it to communication.
- Describe two dogs playing in the park – now compare this to friendship.
- Describe smoking a cigarette – now compare this to romance.
- Complete the phrase: 'Life is like a ...'
  (be original – no Forrest Gump references, please!)
- Close a random object or noun and compare it to an abstract noun (see 'Prompts' section).

Mistakes

Sometimes your mind fills in something you've only partially heard or seen with hysterical results – you tune in to a conversation halfway through, or someone asks you a question and you mishear it. As well as laughing at these mix-ups, use these misinterpretations to generate new ideas.

Notebooks

Notebooks are a vital tool for any thinker and artist. I don't often give "musts" but you MUST keep something with you at all times to record ideas in. My phone works best for me since I have it with me everywhere I go. With the best of intentions, I had a Filofax for a short time and kept everything in there – credit cards, wallet, to-do list and notebook, but in the end it was just too bulky and awkward. And I couldn't stand the thought of losing all my writing ideas in the pub or taxi (credit cards can be replaced, after all, but inspiration cannot).

Ideally, you'll write using these ideas as soon as possible after you've found them. There have been plenty of times I've looked over old suggested titles or first lines and wondered what on earth I'd been thinking about that day. Strike while the iron's hot and sparks will fly.

While it can be a helpful memory aid to note things in a scientific way, historically accurate lists of facts don't always make for the most creative or engaging writing. Joan Didion suggests it is more useful for a writer to describe things not as they are, but as they seem, as they feel, imaginatively, creatively, using your subconscious to help.

> So the point of my keeping a notebook has never been, nor is it now, to have an accurate factual record of what I have been doing or thinking... How it felt to me: that is getting closer to the truth about a notebook.
> – Joan Didion

What to note down:
- whatever you're thinking about right now
- snatches of dialogue
- descriptions of settings
- story ideas
- story titles
- opening lines
- closing lines

Anything you like! You don't have to show anyone else your notes unless you want to. They're completely yours to do with as you will. So enjoy the freedom. Draw, scribble, tear them up, even burn them (if you're feeling brave and carefree enough – I'm not sure I could, but more power to you if you can).

Open-Mindedness

If you're open-minded, you're less likely to shut down or shut out a new idea when it occurs, no matter how crazy it might initially seem. Take care not to reject or criticise an idea that arises. This immediately slams the door to opportunity.

Opposites

Choose an adjective from the end of this book and use it and its opposite to play with ideas.

Go further: Darkness and light. Think darkness and inspiration. Think darkness and day. Go with whatever comes to mind. There's no right or wrong here, don't censor yourself. The more ideas the better, it doesn't matter what they are.

Go even further. Look at the nouns and abstract nouns, go through the same process with these. Remember, this might be challenging initially – don't shrink from challenge, have fun with it! You might pleasantly surprise yourself.

For example: pursuit and flight. Pursuit and capture. Entrapment. Pursuit and relaxation. Pursuit and freedom. I'm sure you can do better. Go for it.

Originality

Consider things in a new way by using new words, new contexts and new perspectives. Challenge your old assumptions in order to think up new concepts.

Ask yourself open questions that expand your creativity, such as:

Life is…?

Trees are an example of…?

Luc de Brabandere, in his TED talk, *Reinventing Creative Thinking*, suggests describing whatever topic you're considering in as many different ways as possible – but without using the first five words that come to mind. He uses his example of helping a champagne company think up new marketing ideas. By avoiding their exhausted ideas and concepts, they realised their business was about helping people celebrate. They reframed their business context from the product itself to the concept of special occasions. And published a book about how to deliver a speech – which was a great hit.

By reframing a question or putting a topic in a new context, you will be more able to think up fresh and original ideas. This is especially useful when you're stuck in a rut or want to think up something unusual for writing competitions.

People

Make connections between people – perhaps have two characters from your different stories meet and see how they hit it off.

People-watch. Write an imagined history of the first person that grabs your attention. What would happen if they met a person coming the other way?

Question

I have no special talent. I am only passionately curious.
  – Einstein

Ask questions of everything. Who, what, where, when, why and how.

Look up at the stars and not down at your feet. Try to make sense of what you see, and wonder about what makes the universe exist. Be curious.
  – Stephen Hawking

Investigate

Revise or research a topic that fascinates you. Researching a subject can help you find and furnish your settings. Your investigations may reveal some interesting people to base characters on and you may even find whole other worlds to explore.

> **Writers write about their obsessions. Things that haunt them; things they can't forget; stories they carry in their bodies waiting to be released... Your main obsessions have power, they are what you come back to in your writing over and over again.** – Natalie Goldberg

Finding out new things can definitely fire up the creative synapses necessary for writing. Your passions will shine through. However, two notes of warning:

1. Try not to indulge yourself in research to the point that it becomes procrastination.

2. Just because you have knowledge doesn't mean you need to impart it all. Especially if info-dumping impedes the flow of your story or clashes with the voice of the narrative.

Take Care of Yourself

A little bit of self-care goes a long way. Many a moment I could have been writing was ruined because I was too tired or distracted.

Drink (water!) Make sure you're getting plenty of fluids. At least two litres a day. Brain-fog and lethargy are classic signs of dehydration.

Exercise – get that blood pumping! More blood and more endorphins to the brain mean more ideas and increased positivity. Added bonus, you'll be more likely to offset the effects of sitting and writing. You very rarely see a magpie that suffers from spreading-bum syndrome!

Sleep. The better you sleep, the more clearly you'll be able to think and the more motivated you'll likely feel as well. Plus, if you get a really good sleep, you'll be more likely to experience that wonderful half-sleep you get before fully waking up, when you can experience the most vivid, most lucid dreams.

Themes & Issues, Messages & Morality

This is as much a note of caution as it is a suggestion. Generally, it's not a great idea to write (stories at least) using a theme as a jumping-off point: racism, sexism, divorce, politics, religion. These are meaty issues that affect everyone, but writing that's driven by a theme tends to lack depth in its characters, who then become mere tools in your quest to beat your reader over the head with your opinions on a chosen issue.

Writing from theme feels like squeezing toothpaste back into its tube, or sausage meat into a sausage skin. It's difficult to cram a story into a shape that it doesn't want to fit! Besides, what results tends to be fairly patronising.

It's important to free yourself up while writing. It's only by doing so that you'll allow your subconscious to play on the page. Trying to compress a story or poem into conveying a specific message will only constrain your writing and produce a preachy, pretentious piece.

Focus on your characters and setting and story. Allow the theme or message of a story to come out organically. Don't force it.

But... I've included theme here because everything's worth trying and you never know, this might work for you. I'd suggest it as a starting point that you can mind-map from, but remember, don't let theme lead your story – follow your characters.

Treasure Trove

Any *Magpie* moments that you don't get a chance to expand on straight away should be safely stored in your treasure trove. Whether this is on your phone, in a notebook, a purse, or wherever else you've stashed them for the sake of speed and convenience, take them out or transcribe them onto paper as soon as you can.

Consider putting them somewhere that symbolically demonstrates their value and significance to you. Of course it doesn't *have* to be somewhere special. Ian Rankin just puts his notes and clippings into an old manila folder that he goes through before starting a new novel. You could also take pictures on your phone, refer to sketches you've made, doodles, small objects you've held on to, clippings from newspapers and magazines, pictures from adverts and articles – anything and everything.

Rifle through your treasure trove regularly so that the sparkles in there don't tarnish. Use your soft focus, your relaxed gaze as you look them over.

A mixed blessing about the treasure trove is that those things you put into it, those *Magpie* moments that you didn't have time to write about straight away, when you go through them, you might realise that you have no idea now why they once had you so spellbound. This is motivation enough to record them more fully next time, when you're still in that moment of beguilement, rather than leave them to languish.

Treat Yourself

Fill the well that you draw from. Do something new, something interesting, something exciting, something scary, something enriching, something enjoyable. Even something you suspect you'll hate. Julia Cameron calls making time for these experiences 'artist's dates'.

> **Keep human! See people, go places, drink if you feel like it.**
> **– Henry Miller**

You need experience to help open your mind and give you more things to reflect on, to be inspired by.

> **A writer's brain is like a magician's hat. If you're going to get anything out of it, you have to put something in it first.**
> **– Louis L'Amour**

See the suggestions at the end of this book for some ideas and make a list of your own.

Read

Make a point of reading something new every day. Poetry, if at all possible. Short stories. A novelist that you admire.

> **If you don't have time to read, you don't have the time (or the tools) to write. Simple as that.**
> **– Stephen King**

Keep a notebook handy. If what you're reading is really good, then you will probably feel your *Magpie* stir.

Synchronicity

Notice when coincidences happen. When you meet a person you've just been thinking about. When you see a programme on television about a place you liked to visit as a child and then your significant other suggests going there for a day trip. When you're starting a book called *Magpie Mind* and then a magpie taps through your living room window at you, take note (true story). Pay attention. The universe is telling you something.

What If...

Writers, especially novel writers, explore what-ifs in their writing. Stephen King writes most of his novels using what-ifs to start him off.

> ...these were all situations which occurred
> to me – while showering, while driving,
> while taking my daily walk – and which I
> eventually turned into books.
> – Stephen King

If you ever stop to consider what might happen if you do a certain thing, or what might have happened if you had made a different decision, or what you might be capable of, then take those questions down and write stories that answer them. It's a low-risk way of exploring some of those infinite alternate realities.

> I write to give myself strength. I write to
> be the characters that I am not. I write to
> explore all the things I'm afraid of.
> – Joss Whedon

'What if…' is pure gold for speculative writers. What might have happened if Dorothy had followed the red brick road rather than the yellow? What would happen if the earth stopped spinning and gravity suddenly stopped holding us safe and tight to the ground?

Workshops and Groups

Writing workshops and groups can be very useful to budding and stalled writers, both. A good one will help you experiment with your writing in different ways. A great workshop will build your confidence as well.

Meeting and discussing your processes with other writers will inevitably help with your own practice. They'll provide inspiration and encouragement too, as others share their unique methods. Workshops provide important benefits to writers of all levels: feedback, guidance, an audience, and a community.

Poetry starts with Word Worms. They bounce around your head. Even in sleep. They harass you, are relentless until they see themselves on the page. If you are lucky they bed down, but the reality is they take a while to settle.

My prose writing is character driven. Most narrative arrives complete and it is a race to get it down. I love people. Talking with or watching people. Often it will be my interpretation of them as a character that is the result, not verbatim.

When I was in the Shetland archives, researching trade between Unst and Bergen in 1530, six lines about a Danish noble and some children jumped out at me. I knew that a great story sat behind.

Smooth Your Feathers

Especially for those of us who enjoy a busy schedule, being on the go all the time can be exhilarating – but it can also be very distracting. Squeezed between appointments and projects, your mind is left with scant time to focus on what to make for dinner, never mind dream up something creative.

It's essential that in between your busy times you find time to relax. For your own good and for the good of your imagination. There are numerous things you could do to help quiet your inner chatter. Some of my favourites include mindfulness meditation, walking, swimming, listening to music and dancing. Fully immerse yourself in a luxury, whether it's a bubble bath or eating a bowl of fresh strawberries and cream or watching the sun rise. Take yourself on what Julia Cameron calls an 'artist's date' and enjoy some small indulgences, anything that takes you out of yourself (your Self) and into a little peace and quiet. Shut yourself off from everything else around you and appreciate each and every sensation you encounter.

You'll not be able to listen to anything outside yourself unless your logical, thinking mind is quiet. So, find – or make – time and space in your schedule for time and space.

Time and Space

Guy Claxton, in *Hare Brain, Tortoise Mind*, describes different kinds of thinking: the logical, analytical intelligent conscious, and the emotional, intuitive intelligent unconscious. The intelligent unconscious is the *Magpie Mind*. It's imaginative and playful. Rather than dealing with a problem logically, if you give yourself time to ruminate over a problem in a relaxed way, it will meander around and look at the issue from different perspectives. It is in this state, according to Claxton, that our most creative ideas occur.

> **During periods of relaxation after concentrated intellectual activity, the intuitive mind seems to take over and can produce the sudden clarifying insights which give so much joy and delight.**
> **– Fritjof Capra (Physicist)**

Shakespeare called it 'the spell in which imagination bodies forth the forms of things unknown'. Einstein said that, as well as staring into space, some of his best ideas occurred when he was taking a shower.

Nobel Prize winner Leo Szilliard revealed that the concept of a nuclear chain reaction came to him while he was waiting at some London traffic lights. So build incubation time into your process, time in which your mind can mull over a problem while you're doing something else.

Martin Amis calls this crucial stage in his writing process 'marination': leaving the idea to rest so that all the flavours can infuse. Frame the problem up front in your logical mind, then go about your routine. In the background, the synapses in your brain will continue to fire away and create connections in order to help solve your problem. Quite often, the solution will pop up out of nowhere. It's all about getting yourself into the right frame of mind, which means giving your intelligent unconscious the chance to do its work.

Clear little pockets of space and time in your schedule to let inspiration happen.

> **Imagination needs moodling – long, inefficient happy idling, dawdling and puttering.**
> **– Brenda Ueland**

Slow Down

Focus on one thing at a time. Focus completely. Zoom in, look at the tiny details, now zoom out and look at the space around it. Think about how it relates to the world. Consider bigger ideas.

Switch your phone off. Switch your television off. Separate yourself off from as many of your immediate gratification monkey's tools as you can. Devote your entire attention to the task at hand. This will help you open up to your intuition (or Muse).

> To find the universal elements enough; to find the air and the water exhilarating; to be refreshed by a morning walk or an evening saunter... to be thrilled by the stars at night; to be elated over a bird's nest or a wildflower in spring - these are some of the rewards of the simple life.
> – John Burroughs

Having a *Magpie Mind* is about being open to the experiences around you and inside you. Pay full and appreciative attention to individual ideas as they arise.

Watch and Wait

Perch yourself on a branch somewhere and look around. Use the examples from 'Filling Your Nest' to help you if you like, but on the whole:

> **Slow down and enjoy life. It's not only the scenery you miss by going too fast - you also miss the sense of where you are going and why.**
> **– Eddie Cantor**

Take a step back, away from the front of your mind. Breathe. Relax your eyes, your shoulders, gaze around you with a soft focus, look downward, listen. When your ears perk up, or your attention is snagged by some passing glimmer of magic, observe and marvel.

> **Develop interest in life as you see it; in people, things, literature, music - the world is so rich, simply throbbing with rich treasures, beautiful souls and interesting people. Forget yourself.**
> **– Henry Miller**

Trust in this process, so innate to all of us, and something will happen.

Fly Above the Clouds

> We need to be willing to let our intuition
> guide us, and then be willing to follow
> that guidance directly and fearlessly.
> – Shakti Gawain

When something does call to you, enjoy it to the fullest. Stretch your soul out to explore the corners and edges of the experience. Like a cat, rub your awareness up against the textures of a street or forest or wherever you find yourself. Roll your tongue over the vowels and consonants in a poem or song you're listening to.

Hum the notes of music or a conversation deep in your chest. Observe thoughts and emotions and insights as they arise within you.

These are the times when, in the midst of the mundane, you are being called on to create a more powerful, meaningful experience. Respect that and you will be rewarded in ways you may never fully comprehend.

> [The arts] are a very human way of
> making life more bearable. Practicing an
> art, no matter how well or badly, is a way
> to make your soul grow, for heaven's sake.
> – Kurt Vonnegut

Transcending Normality

What I'm suggesting you do is discover the secret that thinkers and artists have known for millennia:

> **The only real valuable thing is intuition.**
> – Einstein

It's in this intuitive mindset that you find your zest for writing, for life. It's in that spark of inspiration where you'll find joy. That joy of creation. That whole-hearted impetus. The spark that explodes – or fades away. Feed it! Don't abandon it, don't suffocate it with doubt. Note it down, fan it with your attention until it ignites into something roaring and hot and alive!

> **The first thing a writer should be is excited. He should be a thing of fevers and enthusiasms.** – Ray Bradbury

Using your *Magpie Mind* isn't about escaping life, though that can be fun too. It's about fully experiencing and appreciating what's already present in your life. It's about being happy, relaxed and joyful, open to participating in the worlds around you and within you, connecting with your intuition and other people.

It's about enriching your day with new perspectives and insights. Every experience of inspiration has the potential to revitalise you, if you let it.

Wonder

The *Magpie Mind* process is all about spontaneous observation and immersing yourself in the inspired moment. I'm asking you to rediscover your childish wonder.

> **Every child is an artist. The problem is**
> **how to remain an artist once he grows up.**
> **– Pablo Picasso**

When your attention is grabbed and held by an experience, it's your inner child tugging on your sleeve. How cruel, then, would it be to shut that child out? How soul-destroying.

> **He who can no longer pause to wonder**
> **and stand rapt in awe, is as good as dead;**
> **his eyes are closed. – Albert Einstein**

Like a child, that instinct is much more likely to return to you if you pay it the grateful attention that it deserves. And of course you will benefit as well.

> **We gazed dreamily at the Milky Way and once in a while caught some shooting stars. Times like these gave me the opportunity to wonder and ask all those very basic questions. That sense of awe for the heavens started there.**
> – Kalapana Chawla

Your *Magpie Mind* is ultimately useful because the spontaneous inspiration that it offers completely bypasses your critical voice.

You can avoid all your doubts and fears by simply immersing yourself in the gift that the moment brings.

Tom Leonard

'We are alchemists who would extract the essence of perpetual youth from dust and ashes, tempt coy Truth in many light and airy forms from the bottom of her well, and discover one crumb of comfort or one grain of good in the commonest and least-regarded matter that passes through our crucible. Spirits of past times, creatures of imagination, and people of today are alike the objects of our seeking, and, unlike the objects of search with most philosophers, we can insure their coming at our command.'

(Charles Dickens, From Master Humphrey's Clock, the weekly periodical the young Dickens launched in 1840 after writing Nicholas Nickleby)

Suggested by Tom Leonard: 'This from the opening section of the first volume may be of use to you, though only a great writer like Dickens could sustain it.'

Magpie in the Mirror

As well as being one of the most dapper species on the planet, magpies may well be one of the most intelligent. Alongside elephants, dolphins and some apes, they're one of the few species who have the capacity for self-awareness. They can, for example, recognise themselves in a mirror.

Follow their example and reflect on yourself and your writing process. This can be incredibly valuable, as shown in Henriette Anne Klauser's recommendation of writing a regular Process Log (see 'Panning for Gold'). One advantage of doing so is that it becomes easier to identify your own personal style.

Something I often hear from workshoppers is the concern that they feel they cannot write because they have not found their voice yet. I often answer, 'Who else's voice would you use?'

Look back over your life. Consider your experiences and how they have affected you. Perhaps in a diary, perhaps through *Wellspring* writing.

Find your humanity and engage your readers.

> **What do you think of the world? You, the prism, measure the light of the world; it burns through your mind to throw a different spectroscopic reading onto white paper than anyone else can throw. Let the world burn through you.**
> **– Ray Bradbury**

What moves you to tears, to indignation? What do you desire more than anything else in the world? What do you loathe? What do you fear? What do you cherish? Witnessing what excites you is a first step in finding that which will animate your writing. Discovering what is most important to you will energise your writing with characters and narrators with depth and motivations that help them move and act of their own accord.

> Find a character... who will want something or not want something, with all his heart. Give him running orders. Shoot him off. Then follow as fast as you can go.
> – Ray Bradbury

Originality depends upon you trusting your instincts and impressions as they happen. When you write, you're completely on your own. That's both a scary and a wonderful place to be. You're in the perfect position to find your own original perspective on the world. Finding your 'voice' is really more about finding your originality – but your writing will be original anyway, fuelled by your own distinct preoccupations.

> The unconscious is smart... The trick is to bring it out, get it down... getting it down is what the writer really cares about, setting

> down what the writer himself notices, as
> opposed to what any fool might notice, is
> all that is meant by the originality of the
> writer's eye.
> – John Gardner

Paying attention to your magpie and what it tells you will clue you in to what you could, and perhaps should, write about.

The more an idea grabs you, the more it preoccupies you, the more important it is to write about. Anyone who has been woken up at 4am on a summer morning by the non-too melodic machine-gun rattle of a parliament of magpies will attest to the fact that magpies have a distinctive – and insistent – voice. There's no ignoring it.

The Self and Yourself – Ego and Identity

Finding yourself (your Self) means finding what is common to all, it's about exploring humanity. But don't fall too much in love with the stories you tell your Self about yourself. Look outward. Naval-gazing won't take you far in life. Besides, there are so many interesting things out there to look at and learn from.

> **Develop interest in life as you see it; in people, things, literature, music – the world is so rich, simply throbbing with rich treasures, beautiful souls, and interesting people. Forget yourself.**
> **– Henry Miller**

Be warned – don't identify too much with the idea of 'your voice'. On the map of your writing journey, here be monsters. Namely your Ego – with a capital E.

Ego and narcissism are dangerous temptations that inevitably get in the way of you receiving and acting upon helpful feedback. Try not to attach too much to your ideas as your own. It will be less painful when you come to edit your work.

It's more helpful to consider the idea that these initial words and ideas are not yours. You're just the filter – and the less you get in the way, the more magic the ideas often have.

> **The author must keep his mouth shut when his work starts to speak.**
> **– Frederich Nietzsche**

NB: That's not to say you can't be miffed if someone plagiarises your work.

Once you've polished up your initial idea into the finished product, you will have put a great deal of valuable knowledge, experience and time into your writing – for someone to simply steal that isn't fair. Or legitimate. Plagiarisers beware – you're cheating yourself of all the fun of discovering something of your own – simply because you're afraid that you can't do it. Give yourself a good shake and realise that you already have something of worth to offer. There's no need to steal from others.

> **Your passion will protect you from slanting or imitation.**
> **– Ray Bradbury**

Often we imitate others because we feel insecure about our own writing. We don't feel our writing, without the flavour of another's, will ever be good enough. We don't even start writing our novel or our poem or short story because we doubt our ability to do the idea justice. We don't think we'll ever be as good as other, 'proper' writers.

But we have very little influence over what ideas we receive and what ideas we don't. We don't have control over our magpie – nor should we try to exert any. Magpies are wild after all, and should be free.

> **We do not choose our subjects.**
> **They choose us.**
>   **– Gustave Flaubert**

Who else can write your idea the way you can? We've all been tempted, when moved by something we've read, to write like other authors, but if you try to imitate other writers your writing will lack instinct, authenticity, and passion.

So there's no need to become attached to the idea of your 'voice.' Such a thing is not fixed anyway. Bear in mind that your individual style will evolve as you grow in experience and knowledge. You can only write in the moment you're in. You can always re-write in the future, but even then, if you come back to your piece, you'll want to change it to reflect what you know in that moment.

That doesn't mean you shouldn't edit it, but what it does mean is that a piece of writing is never actually finished. You will just have to learn to let go of it at some point, otherwise you'll never write anything new!

Letting go will help prevent you from identifying too strongly with your writing. The truly great moments of writing happen when ideas flow through us, not necessarily from us. From moments when you are awake and open.

Henry James called the spark of inspiration a *domnée*, a gift, something you receive. What you're expressing isn't, I believe, yours anyway. Ideally, what you're writing is something that flows through you from somewhere else. You're simply the conduit.

> We are the instrument more than the author of our work.
> – Julia Cameron

So relax and let it happen. Don't force it.

When you're inspired by something, that's when the opportunity for creative flow is presenting itself to you. It's when a chink in the wall between normal life and a mysterious place opens up and something sparkles through it.

> Inspiration may be a form of superconsciousness, or perhaps of subconsciousness – I wouldn't know. But I am sure it is the antithesis of self-consciousness.
> – Aaron Copeland

Writing as soon as inspiration hits, or taking notes as soon as it happens, means you allow your subconscious to ascend from the depths, to bubble up in blips of oxygen that keep your writing fresh, and animate it with life.

Going beyond yourself, transcending your Self, means you can fly free, beyond your fears, beyond your doubts, petty jealousies, criticisms and resentments and excuses that hold you back.

> **For anyone who loves intensely lives not in himself but in the object of his love, and the further he can move out of himself into his love, the happier he is.**
>   **– Erasmus**

Alan Bissett

The feeling, the moment of inspiration, is what we as writers live for. It's addictive, like coming up, the quicksilver sensation of something shifting, clicking in the brain, unmistakeable, impossible to plan for. But you know it when it's happening: something glimpsed or overheard or felt or experienced that has a certain texture from which we weave fiction or poetry.

Sitting in bed earlier this evening with the baby, my partner and I, both writers: she's peering into the bottle of white fluid she's just expressed, calculating the amount she's already given the baby and how much more he needs later and she says, 'Hmm, the maths of milk.'

The two of us just looked at each other and both said at the same time, 'I'm having it.' The Maths of Milk. What a title. We just knew. Swirl that around in your consciousness and see what settles: what story, what characters, what themes? Well, let's write it and find out.

I'm an atheist, but when people talk about inspiration being 'divine' I get it. You feel somehow more connected to the world. Your senses are heightened. Your ego seems to disappear and you tap into something larger than yourself, a similar experience which we have during transcendental meditation, or prayer, or drug trips.
Then comes the more prosaic business of committing words to the page, in the right order, with the right weight to them, trying to do justice to that moment of inspiration, capture it, turn it into something which shape which the world will recognise.

That's the hard part. But nothing happens without the easy part.

Of Magpies
& Monkeys

In *Wellspring* we touched on the idea of instant gratification monkeys. These mischievous little creatures want to divert you away from activities involving long-term effort and tempt you instead towards those that will give you a bit of cheap, lazy, short-term fun.

When an insight or a moment of inspiration glimmers at you, you'll be tempted to go after it, but may hesitate if you're busy with another project.

At these times there is every chance that your *Magpie Mind* and Monkey Mind may overlap. They'll both chatter away to you with suggestions – but how are you to tell inspiration from procrastination? How do you distinguish fool's gold from true treasure? After all, the moments of insight that this book focuses on also provide 'quick and easy' moments of inspired joy.

One question to ask is: do your ideas occur when you're in a key stage of drafting or editing one of your creative projects? If so, take them down very briefly and come back to them as soon as you've finished your poem or short story or chapter. Or if the chatter is loud and insistent and just won't let you go, then go ahead and write it.

Get it down in more detail and then return to your original project as soon as you can.

These lightbulb moments are vitally important to

the creative process as they bypass the negative and critical thoughts that buzz around in your mind and take you to a moment of calm, of insight, of joy – if you'll let them. Having a *Magpie Mind* is about letting your subconscious break through, about chinking open a crack in your logical mind through which you can let the *Wellspring* flow.

While the Monkey Mind is the monster at the gate, the *Magpie Mind* waits to lift you over the wall.

> **Logic will get you from A to B. Imagination will take you everywhere.**
> **– Einstein**

Ultimately we write or create, because

    a) we enjoy it

    b) we can't help ourselves

We've all been seduced by ideas in the past, ideas that burst forth in our minds and nag us you until we get them out, onto the page. You've been seduced by the potential of a brainwave – a concept that could, someday, be truly great, if you ever had the courage to sit down and work through it fully.

That moment of inspiration has tremendous energy.

It gives your writing impetus, a jet-booster thrust to propel your creativity to new heights. Your inner Critic or Martyr usually dispel these, pushing them away in favour of more pressing responsibilities. But I would suggest that *Magpie* moments are in fact the most valuable element of an artist's craft.

Ray Bradbury believed that zest and gusto are the most important qualities for us to have in life, without which we can only be 'half a writer'. So stop beating yourself up for being distracted by a shiny thing. If you're going to write, you might as well enjoy yourself. Follow your instincts, follow your passions. Writing doesn't need to be all tortured-artist experience.

> **The creation of something new is not accomplished by the intellect but by the play instinct.**
> – Carl Jung

No matter how silly, how insane, how childish or ludicrous your ideas may initially seem, note them down. Record them and react to them. Giggle, weep, fume, blush. It doesn't matter if they barely make sense to you now. Let them emerge and treasure them.

> Poetry often enters through the window
> of irrelevance.
>   – M.C. Richards

Magpie-Minding, like *Wellspringing*, reminds you that you *can* do this. There is the potential within you for an infinite flow of ideas. Some will be daft, some will be brilliant.

> The author of genius does keep 'til his last breath the spontaneity, the ready sensitiveness of a child, the 'innocence of eye' that means so much to the painter, the ability to respond freshly and quickly to new scenes, and to old scenes as though they were new... and always to see 'the correspondences between things' of which Aristotle spoke two thousand years ago.
>   – Dorothea Brande

It's important not to stifle your *Magpie Mind* as you might your instant gratification monkeys. An instant gratification monkey's chatter is designed to distract you away from your long-term creative goals. The *Magpie Mind's* fascination, however, can be used to help give your process a vitality. One draws you away, one draws you on.

Desire urges me on, as fear bridles me.
– Giordano Bruno

Stay open to these spontaneous surges of inspiration in order to furnish your nest with treasures to write about. *Wellspring* writing, or free-flow writing – in which you sit down to the blank page and write, write, write – is a process of discovery. So is developing a *Magpie Mind.* You'll encounter new ideas all the time and these spark your imagination with electricity and light.

Emma Mooney

The Spark

The word inspiration infers that some-thing soulful, or perhaps even magical, is involved in the writing process. Don't let this put you off. All we're talking about here is where the ideas for a story or a poem come from.

The spark that ignites an idea, an image, or a thought in your mind can come from any one of the million images, sounds or smells our brain experiences in a single day.

You may wish to try and capture something as familiar as the smell of freshly mown grass on a summer's evening, or perhaps the sound of waves crashing against rocks. Some people would argue these are clichéd but remember that, for you, each experience is unique. And your voice, too, is as individual as the swirls on the shells you bring home in your pockets. Don't feel compelled to find something new to write about. Begin with whatever is in your head ... or heart.

A Warning:
The Gilded Cage

This book is for those writers, artists, thinkers and innovators who prefer to wait for inspiration to strike before sitting down to work.

In this chapter, however, I caution against simply waiting. That way lies doom for any aspiring creator – if you want to be more than a hobbyist (which is fine, honestly, no judgement, we all have hobbies). If you want to take your craft seriously, then you need to turn up for it regularly. It takes active participation.

> Amateurs sit and wait for inspiration, the rest of us just get up and go to work.
> – Stephen King

Of course if we languish long enough, inspiration might eventually arise. But honestly, do you just want to wait? Why not encourage it? The theories and strategies in this book are here to help you create more of these moments.

> To be a writer is to sit down at one's desk in the chill portion of every day, and to write; not waiting for the little jet of the blue flame of genius to start from the breastbone - just plain going at it, in pain and delight.
> – John Hersey

Becoming over-reliant on the idea that you need inspiration to begin writing is a form of procrastination. And it's dangerous. Often, in times of stress and ex-haustion, it just doesn't happen. This, for the creatively occupied, can be agonising. By not actively engaging with the process, you run the risk of feeling that you have lost your imagination; you run the risk of developing imposter syndrome.

Energy and persistence conquer all things.
– Benjamin Franklin

You *can* decide to go hunting for inspiration rather than wait for it to find you. Ideas are everywhere, inside and around you. You just have to adjust your inner radio so it's more sensitive to ideas of all frequencies and strengths.

Developing a Magpie Mind is about opening yourself to revelation, rather than shutting out that part of yourself. Of course it's about spontaneity as well, but that's not to suggest you should wait for it to happen. Look out for those glints of something special that will add zest to your writing. Later you can learn the craft of polishing, but you must have something interesting to start with. To be a good writer, you need first to develop the habit of paying attention to that glimmer of an idea and transcribing it as well as you can onto the page. Don't worry about the literary 'quality' of it – just get it down as soon as you can to increase the chances of capturing it as truly as possible.

> **The true alchemists do not change lead into gold; they change the world into words.**
> **– William H. Gass**

What often puts people off writing, or puts them off sharing their writing, is the idea that they don't have the technical knowledge to write 'well'. Don't be sidelined by a lack of confidence. Craft can be learned, but if you don't have an indefinable energy in your initial idea, then your writing will lack passion, humour and humanity. It will plod along – tedious not only for you as the writer (in which case, why even bother?) but for any reader as well.

Looking out for these special moments in daily life will help you realise your unique voice. Discovering and nurturing your talent is one side of the creative coin. You can learn how to bring it out of yourself. This is the first stage of the process.

On the other side of the coin is having the discipline

to explore your ideas thoroughly, with the knowledge and experience of your craft. This you can learn and hone as you go. Inspiration is just the beginning. But without a beginning, you'll not get far.

> **Nothing in this world can take the place of persistence. Talent will not: nothing is more common than unsuccessful men with talent.**
> **– Calvin Coolidge**

I don't need ideas for poems – I just need a world.

As the years drift by I've come to feel that, for me at least, writing poetry isn't about having ideas for poems. I don't set about dragging concepts and ideas from the depths of my soul or some abstract nether realm of consciousness. Instead, it's a question of attention, of keeping an eye (and an ear) on the world around me, whether that's a cormorant opening its wings, the glimmer of rain on a garage roof or a Joni Mitchell song on the radio. Sometimes this attention feels so intense it amounts to a kind of deep alertness, akin to rapture. At others it's just a glimpse of something or an overheard snatch of sound that buries itself in the memory and takes root.

No doubt the intellect or subconscious or soul – call it what you will – is involved in

*this process, as are all the 'ideas' I've
absorbed about poetry and about the world
from reading so many poets. But it's the
world itself that matters. 'No ideas but in
things' as William Carlos Williams said,
which to my mind is pretty much the same
thing as saying that poetry is primarily a
response – sometimes confused, sometimes
passionate, sometimes revelatory – to the
things of the earth (and beyond). In this
sense, I sometimes think of language itself
as a kind of sense, a way of exploring the
universe from the prosaic to the sublime.
Of course, we would all want a response
to be celebratory, and perhaps poetry has
the edge over prose fiction in this respect.
It doesn't depend on conflict in the same
way. But the notion of poetry as response
holds true for more testing subject matter
as well. War poetry (and political poetry
more generally) has all the more bite if it
is a poetry of witness and experience – not
just pious moralising.*

Of course, we all heave a set of values, of assumptions and opinions about good and bad, beautiful and ugly, sacred and profane, which help to shape our view of the world. But it's not primarily the poet's job to impose these views through their poems. The writing of a poem may challenge what the poet thinks or open up new avenues of thought. It's for this reason that I try to listen out for what the poem itself wants to say, rather than what I thought I wanted it to say. In other words, a poem trusts its reader entirely, its writer not that much, even when they are one and the same person.

So poetry is a means for writer and reader to make sense of the world. But there is another respect in which the poet is concerned with 'making sense'. A poem is a made thing. It isn't just the instinctive blurting out of emotion (though it can be made to look like this). The poet still needs to use judgment, to try to practice their craft well. Robert Frost famously said that poetry is a 'fresh look and a fresh listen' but it's my job to evoke that freshness through craft and technique and form. Through words themselves. The world deserves nothing less.

In the end, I guess it's too evasive, and maybe disingenuous, to say that poems don't contain ideas. But the ideas come through the making of the poem, not before it. It's the poet's alertness to nature and culture and memory and people and things - to stuff that happens - that first nudges, or compels, a poet to write. And that's why I want my poems to be as full of cormorants and rain as they are of ideas.

Resistance

Once you've made time for your creativity, you've already begun to change. You've made a commitment to allow more inspiration into your life. You're sending a signal to your subconscious that you will respect and nurture the ideas it gives you. The next step is to make more time for your writing and grow those seeds of creativity.

This is the scary bit, the bit we all balk at.

How to do our initial idea justice? This clean, pure, perfect flash of an idea, untempered by your own doubts, failings and inadequacies?

Whereas *Wellspring* suggested writing quickly, now you might want to experiment with writing in a quieter, more leisurely way. Be kind, considerate and patient with yourself. But above all, write.

> **Don't be nervous. Work calmly, joyously, recklessly on whatever is in hand.**
> **– Henry Miller**

Ride the Updraft

By using the impetus of the moment when an idea first hits you, you bypass any resistance you might usually have. By immediately following your inspiration, it becomes much easier to resist inertia or the temptation to edit your work because you're so caught up in the … flow.

There's no fight, there's no need to force it.

In this moment, it is easy to ignore your Martyr. Your Martyr who might otherwise succeed in convincing you how important it is to wash the dishes right now, to vacuum the carpets, anything to divert you away from your writing. That's your insecurities creating a convenient distraction.

Instead, listen to the siren call of your Muse. That's your Magpie singing to you. All you have to do is sit down, put pen to paper and write.

Resistance against your higher calling often happens, usually in the form of some immediate gratification that will tempt you away from your long-term aspirations. Art, exercise, healthy eating – anything that is good for you – requires long-term change, effort and discipline.

The more important it is to you, the more resistance you'll put in your own way. The types of things that will tempt you away: social media, television, trashy reading, housework, sex, socialising – all of these can be healthy, fun and relaxing in balance, but when they are used as procrastination, they're destructive to your creative process.

> **At this point, vices kick in. Dope,**
> **adultery, web surfing.**
> **– Stephen Pressfield**

We are all distracted by quick, easy fixes. The creation of drama, too, and the subsequent feeling that we need to solve it, these are very diverting.

And of course, as discussed in *Wellspring*, at the bottom of procrastination...

...is fear.

That Old Chestnut

It is through admitting to ourselves what we really want (and are afraid of having), that we can battle the impulses so destructive to our creativity – the tyranny of our own inner Critic and the lure of our instant gratification monkey. Both seek to entrap us within our comfort zones.

> **The more scared we are of a work or calling, the more sure we can be that we have to do it.**
> – Stephen Pressfield

Instead of these short-term distractions, focus on what truly makes you happy. If that's writing, drawing, or photography, then dedicate your time to doing that! Don't feed your soul junk, you'll make yourself ill.

Ultimately, if you know that being creative is a major part of your personality, if it fulfils you, then denying that part of yourself can only be self-destructive.

Fear of Failure

Adopting a magpie's mindset is one weapon in your arsenal against the dread of the blank page. By committing to listen when your Magpie notices something, you reduce your worry over running out of ideas because inspiration   always appear. You can't suffer imposter syndrome if you have the evidence there in black and white that you can do it.

Don't worry if your first notes don't do your initial idea justice. All writers feel this way about most of their work:

> **The story is always better than your ability to write it. My belief about this is that if you ever get to the point that you think you've done a story justice, you're in the wrong business.**
> **– Robin McKinley**

Self doubt is only natural. It shows that you value your aspirations and your desire to do well. It will help when you are editing and also keep you humble. Being over-confident is a trap the foolhardy fall into, a trap which stops an artist from being healthily self-critical. Any successful thinker or creator will feel the drive to continually improve their work. But don't let self-doubt stop you in your tracks.

> **A great deal of talent is lost to the world for want of a little courage.**
> **– Sidney Smith**

Fear of Success

It's a strange thought, but the prospect of success can be scary. Some don't feel they deserve it. Some, deep down, are comfortable with the way things are.

Success means your life will change. Change is often frightening when we think about it. Sometimes we'd rather sit back and complain about the present and do nothing to confront the challenges of a brave new world.

Pursuing success means risking disappointment. It can cause you to come into conflict with difficult expectations – both those you hold and those others hold of you. What if it's not everything you hoped it would be? Perhaps that old adage *be careful what you wish for* rings in your mind whenever you think about the possibility of leading the life you've always thought you wanted.

Success can actually be traumatic. Those voices that have been telling you all your life that you couldn't – or shouldn't – create, the voices of authority figures such as parents, teachers, even 'friends' - success will mean proving all of them wrong. The very basis of your present existence, your identity, those beliefs you've held about why you can't and you shouldn't create could actually be wrong.

What if your success alienates some people you are close to? You could risk inducing jealousy or competitiveness in those very people whose opinions you've always respected. But then, if they cannot support your achievements, are they really adding any value to your life at all?

Move on. With your fresh energy and approach to life, you'll inevitably find a new circle that can celebrate rather than resent your accomplishments.

Actively deciding to accept these flashes of inspiration from your subconscious helps you avoid victimhood. If you're getting ideas, there's no reason you can't or shouldn't create. There's no reason you couldn't have been creating and thinking for yourself for a long, long time.

You're not trying to fly to the moon here, at least not yet. Breathe. Relax. You're simply letting yourself enjoy, awe and wonder. If that leads to a ground-breaking discovery in rocket propulsion some day, then brilliant! When you're ready, once your innovations have been trialled extensively, then by all means: set a course for the stars.

Alternatives to Failure

> Knowing trees, I understand the meaning of patience. Knowing grass, I can appreciate persistence.
> – Hal Borland

Here's a secret that might terrify you – but will also set you free:

...you will fail.

If you're lucky, you'll experience a few little failures along your journey. If you're very lucky, you'll experience some tremendous failures too.

> A man's errors are his portals of discovery.
> – James Joyce

You'll encounter difficulties, rejection, criticism. Shore yourself up against these by enjoying the ride of the learning curve. Remind yourself why this matters to you and why you're really doing it.

Then keep doing it.

> **If you want to succeed, double your
> failure rate.**
> – Thomas Watson, founder of IBM

You'll get more ideas and not all of them will be wonderful, but you'll enjoy receiving them and going through the process of filtering and exploring them.

> **Ours is a culture and a time as
> immensely rich in trash as it is in
> treasures.**
> – Ray Bradbury

Sifting through the trash and treasures you've produced is an essential stage of creating. And when you're sifting, how do you judge if something is worth developing? Trust your instincts: does it excite you? Can you lose yourself in it? Does it make your soul sing? If the answer to any of these questions is yes, then do it. Trust yourself and follow where your intuition leads. The rewards are enormous.

One day, when you're ready, when you're brave enough, resilient enough, you'll start to work more on your ideas and present them to others for feedback. Then you'll redraft and redraft some more.

> ...let's take a long look at that faintly
> repellent word WORK. It is, above all,
> the word about which your career will
> revolve for a lifetime. Beginning now you
> should become not its slave, which is too
> mean a term, but its partner.
> – Ray Bradbury

Editing, shaping and redrafting can be a long slog, but also a rewarding process, and a necessary one if you want your art to be the best it can possibly be.

You must resign yourself to the fact that what you write may not ever quite live up to that initial formless idea.

> A poem is never a thought to begin with.
> It is at its best when it is a tantalising
> vagueness.
> – Robert Frost

But it is during the search for perfection that we learn. Even if, as with the end of a rainbow, you may actually reach it, the adventure of looking for it is an essential part of the process and is how your voice and skills continuously evolve. Just don't strive so much for perfection that you let frustration put you off working. Some artists and writers will hit a brick wall when their efforts haven't produced the ideal that they initially set out to create. A little more patience and persistence is often useful.

> **And now that you don't have to**
> **be perfect, you can be good.**
> **– John Steinbeck**

Bob Dylan once wrote something he called 'a long piece of vomit about twenty pages long'. It was, he said, 'an ill-formed mass of words'. Then he went back to shaping and shifting it around and that 'piece of vomit' eventually formed *Like a Rolling Stone*.

With hard work, patience and persistence, something close to perfection can be achieved. The process of developing your ideas will be explored more deeply in *In a Grain of Sand*. So for the moment, just enjoy the glory and the mystery of your instincts and impulses. Follow your magpie wherever she flies.

Leonie Charlton

A few of the things that inspire me:

Anything written by Deborah Levy.

Faces that have seen a lot of weather.

The designs of love, the draw of sex. Hands dyed red with oak sap. Hands telling other stories, bloody or otherwise. Grey seals singing. Leonard Cohen singing. Laughter. The sound of a cow tearing at grass. A hen harrier flying low and slow and watchful for tiny tremors below. Poems by Norman McCaig. Poems by Kathleen Jamie. Poems. Poems. Poems.

Lichen overwriting rock. Knowing that there is a word in Gaelic for the pattern cloud shadows make on a hillside. Stags, black with peat, roaring through an October nighttime. Sleep. The smell of honeysuckle in June. A man describing how music takes him right to the bone. A woman gently turning her lover away before getting on the airport bus. My children. The smell of horse and the shape of hoof prints. The steadfastness of limpets. A north wind and the peculiar light it brings.

Final Call

Having a *Magpie Mind* is about looking outwith yourself for inspiration, for opportunity. It's about filling your nest until it overflows with treasure.

It's time to open up and explore. Listen out. Look with a gentle gaze. Let the world place you under its spell.

Find and fly with that which moves you. Feel the air under your wings and let it lift you higher.

Each word is a path of transcendence.
– Satre

Remember – this second, right this second, you could be doing what you really want – right this second, you could begin...

Stuart Paterson

a sudden impulse, like a seagull rising

Prompts

Artist's Dates

- horse-riding
- take an art class
- go white-water rafting
- reread your favourite children's book
- listen to music a friend recommended
- listen to classical music
- dance
- list things you love
- go on a train or a bus – anywhere, it doesn't matter
- parachute jump
- send someone a thoughtful card or a gift
- read a new book or poem or short story
- draw the first thing you lay your eyes on

- organise your playlists/make CDs. Include one full of songs that inspire you
- update or renovate your writing/art space
- cloud-watch
- go to a museum
- scribble randomly and find pictures or words in the scribble
- watch a well-regarded movie
- indulge in a guilty pleasure
- cut clippings from a newspaper or magazine, for example – pictures and interesting words and phrases
- go see a play or music event
- go on a random drive – pick roads you've never driven
- plant something
- go on a thrift/charity/vintage store hunt
- go to a spa
- cook something new
- organise your diary – include writing comp-petitions and events
- build a fort!
- play in your closest or favourite play-park

Fill in the Blanks

Sometimes when I wake up too early, instead of lying there awake in bed, I prefer to get up and _____

When I went on holiday, I was going to sunbathe on the beach but was put off by the _____

I'm staying at my in-laws' while we get our boiler fixed. I'm not sure what's worse, no hot water or my father-in-law's _____

My husband was feeling very tired and grumpy, so I sent him off to bed with a _____

My friend's answer-phone message is very unusual, instead of saying 'Please leave a message', she says_____

My wife is always on a diet, so on our anniversary, instead of chocolate I got her_____

My cat will hunt anything. One day she came in from the garden with a _____ in her mouth.

I was so bored last night, I _____

My friend is so terrified of the dentist, when he goes there he _____

My friend is so funny, in her yearbook she was voted most likely to _____

My bridesmaid didn't want to get me a stripper for my hen night. Instead, she _____

To Find Quiet

- go for a walk in the fresh air
- walk barefoot in grass
- watch the sunrise
- read some haiku
- watch the sun set
- visit a forest
- visit a graveyard
- journal before bedtime
- switch your phone or television off for a day
- go somewhere quiet at night, away from streetlight glare, and stare at the stars
- listen to some peaceful classical music
- eat your favourite food in silence. Savour every bite
- declutter your life: both your home and your schedule (do only what needs to be done)
- get up early and enjoy a cup of tea and some *Wellspring* writing before the world wakes up
- curl up in your favourite cozy blanket or pyjamas
- have a bath using your favourite lotions and potions

Proverbs

Consider how you could use each of these as prompts within different genres: romance, adventure, fantasy, sci-fi, etc. Play around with these to make them original in some way.

- a stitch in time saves nine
- a bad workman always blames his tools
- a bird in the hand is worth two in the bush
- pride comes before a fall
- a journey of a 1000 miles begins with a single step
- all good things come to an end
- all that glitters is not gold
- all's fair in love or war
- put your best foot forward
- among the blind, the one-eyed-man is king
- actions speak louder than words
- a fool and his money are soon parted
- an empty vessel makes the most noise
- absence makes the heart grow fonder
- a chain is only as strong as its weakest link
- an eye for an eye, a tooth for a tooth
- an idle mind is the devil's workshop (and great for magpie-minding!)

Five Senses

Consider your five senses, focus on one at a time. Note as much as you can. Change your focus, moving further out from yourself, then closer in. Then choose what made the biggest impression on you and consider what you associate with those observations: ideas, thoughts, opinions, emotions, memories.

Sight: colour, size, texture, movement, shape, lightness, darkness

Sound: volume, tone, voices, musicality, pace, movement, suddenness, gradualness

Taste: textures, sweetness, sourness, bitterness, softness, dryness, chewiness, spiciness, richness

Touch: smoothness, roughness, softness, pliability, temperature

Smell: pungency, fragrance, strength, subtlety

Connections

Mind map, free-associate or *Wellspring* write for each word, then find connections between words from both sides of your pairing:

fire – ice
water – moon
clock – pen
woman – girl
car – tree
body – cloud
wall – ivy
ocean – bird
home – shoe
love – hate
wind – stone
water – mountain
blanket – carpet
man – boy
cat – dog
sun – table
day – work
book – store

People-Watch

Observe a person in detail. Their facial expressions: what might they be thinking about.

Guess at their past, present and future? Their friendships, relationships, fears, hopes and dreams?

What does their clothing suggests about them? And how might it be misleading? And what do your assumptions say about your own values and judgements?

Look at them from different perspectives, sympathetic and unsympathetic. Villify them, sanctify them, humanise them.

Randomiser

Choose a word from the following lists at random.
Free-associate, play around with finding its opposite
or choose a random pair of words to find connections
between:

Abstract Nouns

kindness	wisdom
deceit	reality
love	misery
anger	trust
pride	danger
comfort	childhood
loyalty	fear
courage	hope
honesty	freedom
bravery	friendship
hate	truth
integrity	pleasure
compassion	awe

Adjectives

ambitious	happy	precious
alert	helpless	prickly
alive	hurt	quick
brave	important	quaint
bright	innocent	real
busy	impossible	rich
calm	jolly	scary
clean	joyous	shiny
creepy	jittery	sleepy
dark	kind	tense
dead	lazy	tired
determined	light	tender
elegant	lonely	upset
evil	motionless	unusual
easy	mushy	vast
fair	misty	vivacious
feisty	nasty	wandering
frail	naughty	wicked
fierce	nervous	witty
gleaming	open	wild
graceful	old	xenophobic
gentle	obnoxious	zany

Note of Thanks

To **the many, many writers** who've come to Figment workshops over the years and argued that it's perfectly okay to simply wait for inspiration to hit.

To **Alasdair Gammack** for great conversation.

To **Claire Brunton** and **Alan MacFarlane** for all our chats about writing and early mornings and for taking my nagging with good grace.

To **Charlie Gracie** for taking me under your wing.

To **Sandy Garfunkel** for our chats about characters who speak to you – I agree, writing is a socially acceptable form of schizophrenia.

To **Tom Leonard**, you were always a black pepper crack of education.

To **Janice Galloway** for your inestimable generosity and good grace.

Allan Michie, you were one of the most persistent (stubborn)!

To **Mark**, without whose support this could never have been written.

And to **Riley** – my favourite wee magpie, picking up glimmers of brilliance wherever you go.

Recommended Reading

Zen in the Art of Writing, Ray Bradbury

Headstrong, Tony Buzan

The Artist's Way, Julia Cameron

Hare Brain, Tortoise Mind, Guy Claxton

On Keeping a Notebook, Joan Didion

In Praise of Folly, Erasmus

On Becoming a Novelist, John Gardner

A Temple of Texts, William H. Gass

Writing down the Bones, Natalie Goldberg

On Writing, Stephen King

Essentials of Spontaneous Prose, Jack Kerouac

On Poetry, Glyn Maxwell

The Art of Storytelling, Nancy Mellon

The War of Art, Stephen Pressfield

A Way of Writing, William Stafford

Why Write, Satre

Notes on the Art of Poetry, Dylan Thomas